you are
HERE

you are
HERE

PAUL BRESLIN

TRIQUARTERLY BOOKS
NORTHWESTERN UNIVERSITY PRESS
EVANSTON, ILLINOIS

TriQuarterly Books
Northwestern University Press
Evanston, Illinois 60208-4210

Printed in the United States of America

ISBN 0-8101-5102-2 (CLOTH)
ISBN 0-8101-5103-0 (PAPER)

Library of Congress Cataloging-in-Publication Data

Breslin, Paul.
    You are here / Paul Breslin.
        p. cm.
    ISBN 0-8101-5102-2 (alk. paper) — ISBN 0-8101-5103-0 (pbk. : alk. paper)
    I. Title.
    PS3552.R392 Y68 2000
    811'.6—dc21

                                                    00-010348

CONTENTS

II

ACKNOWLEDGMENTS

I am grateful to the editors of the magazines from which, with various degrees of revision, the following poems are reprinted:

AGNI "In a Rowboat, Once, by Night," "A Visit"

American Poetry Review "Vicissitudes of Orpheus"

American Scholar "Homage to Webern"

Canto "Keepsake"

New Republic "In Order to Be Happy, I Get Depressed"

Ploughshares "Three Poems of Elijah" (parts 1 and 3)

Poetry "Meditations on the Field Museum," "The Return," "You Are Here"

TriQuarterly "Home," "Late Arrival," "The Scale," "The Stairs of the House," "Three Poems of Elijah" (part 2), "To a Friend Who Concedes Nothing," "Two Doors Down"

Virginia Quarterly Review "The Wounds"

I

THE WOUNDS

Wound of the sea. Ships' poultice
ground in its maw. Sky wound
the sun pours through. Seeding
the skin with lesions, sealing
in cataracts eyes that, on first
opening, loved it. Wound

of our bodies, condemned
to extend in space that boils
with corrosive particles—
without a whisper
they drill to the bone.

The tower, forgetting
the years we lifted it
stone by stone,
threw down its shadow—
Spartacus and his followers
jeweled with flies
the length of the Appian Way.

Then one who gave
his palms to the nails
said, *The only defense
is none.* With iron
drawn from his hands,

we fashioned ploughshares,
maces spined
like the morning star,
and instruments
for the torturer's dungeon
under the drains of the tower.

THE SCALE

The man doing life with no chance of parole,
Watching the walls grow visible in the first light,
Thinks how, all over the city, men wake up beside women;
Even the losers get lucky sometimes, but nobody
Gets lucky here, where they put you to make sure
You have no pleasure, and miss it constantly.
The guilt that had seemed almost nothing inside him
They had made solid, so that he could not look
Away from it to take some comfort from the sky
Without seeing bars also.

                    It could have been worse:
One hears that in certain countries, political prisoners
Are locked in boxes too short to lie down in,
Carried down to a cellar, and stacked like so many
Warehouse crates, in one dense tenement
Of tormented flesh soaked in its own excrement.

For someone, somewhere, this is actual; one of those boxes
Is where he is and has to continue being.
If he dreamed of a prison cell
With a bed and a toilet, he would weep bitterly
To wake in his box and find it all a dream.

This is the stone on the far pan of the scale;
Load what you will on the other, it scarcely trembles.

THE STAIRS OF THE HOUSE

Standing halfway up with the vacuum
he noticed that he knew each one,
could tell if a streak of gray was dust
   or a flaw in the grain.

His wife had stripped the paint from the banisters,
sent the spindles out to be dipped,
and together they'd altered the bottom landing's
   awkward shape.

Now, its grain returned to the sunlight,
the creaking oak was more tightly braced.
How many times it had carried them
   up to their rest,

and down to the work of another day.
It seemed a form of gratitude
for all their care, a partnership,
   however mute,

of flesh and the inanimate.
He thought of the impassive face
of the previous owner, who had let
   the place decay,

and before her, the man who poured
concrete divides for the flowerbeds—
hidden by soil now, they blunted
   garden spades—

also the thin, elusive trace
of others, dead beyond retrieval:
the ones who papered the living room
    in dull green floral,

the ones who built the porch enclosure
he'd had to hammer away again.
They were almost a family, and he
    the youngest son,

hating most of their decisions,
grudging the hours of sweat it took
to repair their ubiquitous meddling,
    undo their work;

yet, after quarreling for years,
he came to feel a bond with them:
he and his wife, for reasons still
    unclear to him

(his mother said that his first house
he couldn't remember living in
looked exactly like it, down
    to the floor plan),

had bought it, shaped it to their desire,
fixed what broke as best they could,
worked at their jobs, and raised a child
    to womanhood.

They'd come downstairs for the last time
someday (impossible, but true),
leaving the work of their hands for other
    hands to undo.

IN ORDER TO BE HAPPY, I GET DEPRESSED

If things were really hopeless, I'd relax
instead of wandering around the house
and thinking, What was I supposed to do
today, or any other day I've lived?
Of course we are not poetry—our wives
and friends know better, if we don't. The self
one simply breathes, until the air runs out.
And what does the window hold? The light, that loves us
too impartially; the birds, adrift
where I would fall, and headed somewhere neither
fated nor chosen; trees the sun has pulled
from seeds those birds might eat, their shelter now.
Having nothing to add, I get to work.

NEIGHBORHOOD NINTH

No phone calls, and the mailman hasn't come
to wake the dog, but late in the adagio,
not long before the outburst in the horns,
a police car passes slowly down the street,
then reappears, just as the previous themes
have been dismissed, and joy builds in the brass,
only to be struck down. Precisely when
the bass affirms that *alle Menschen werden
Brüder,* a woman rushes through the courtyard,
waves anxiously toward someone I can't see,
and then four burly cops go past my window,
follow her to her entry, and disappear.

And suddenly the double fugue that marries
the Wingèd Daughter Joy to All the World
is triple, and the third, unwanted theme
is my awareness of the Cops Inside.
One by one, they come back out. The last
has lingered, staring up abstractedly
at nothing, or the trees against the sky.
The stock of his revolver holds the sunlight
darkly, like expensive furniture.

The chorus finishes; the tympanist,
unbound Prometheus, hammers Joy home.

TWO DOORS DOWN

On the front porch, returning late, her son
Is calling up to her to let him in,

And she refuses. So he curses her.
Things usually get violent from here,

But there's a pause, and when she tells
Him he had better shut his mouth or else

She means to kick his sorry-looking ass,
Her tone is strangely close to tenderness,

As if she has to say it, so that he
Can't take forgiveness from her easily.

Unnerved by that slight quaver in her voice,
He needs an answer, something that saves face.

"Bullshit! Fuck it!" he says, over and over,
Caught in a silence that his words can't cover.

DAUGHTER

Where can that small girl hide inside this young woman
   who weighs each word before she speaks,
      shying from the embrace
      she teaches me not to offer?

      Time, though you circle my eyes,
      diminish the strength in my body,
  and send me dreams in black and white only,
these are not the cruelest among your gifts.

THE QUESTION

1968

One March night, late, the air
fogged with thawed snow, someone
behind me, timing his pace to mine

at a distance. I turned, he turned.
When I crossed midblock, where you wouldn't,
he crossed too.

At the curb I was certain,
and turned on my heel:
"Leave me alone, you shit!"

He stopped under a streetlamp, letting me see him:
my height, and skinny. If he wasn't
packing a knife or a gun, it could be all right.

What he carried instead was a question:
"You call me a spic?" "No, *shit*."
He stared, said nothing.

We're close to the river, I thought;
people end up there. Then he made up his mind:
"OK. Just you never call me no spic."

He turned on his heel and left me
standing where I had stopped.
I fumbled through scraps

in my pocket. My heartbeat
was slowing down as my hand
closed, clenching my keys.

BOOK CLUB

1969

Stopping midtown on the long ride from Flushing
to buy Lowell's *Notebook,*
its cover blue of the sky-strip overhead;
the heat coiled in the sidewalks
climbed the airtrough between buildings
so passersby were a boiling mirage.

It seeped down the subways,
filling the tunnels where I rode,
my hair damp on my shoulders
and over my ears. The crammed car
leaned around curves, so that women's breasts
grazed the forearms of men, while the women's faces
looked away and tried to be elsewhere.
Hands groped for balance.

The car slowed; riders
too tired to brake their momentum
threw the rest forward. My hands stopped
on the waist of a huge man
with a flat-top haircut,
who turned, sized me up in a glance, and snapped

KEEP YER HANDS DOWN, FAGGOT!

I slammed the unread poems
about civilization as murder
against the head I could barely reach.

The surge flung us onto the platform,
where we squared off. The crowdstream parted,
as if in a drill it had practiced,
clearing us space to fight.

Then someone (a wiry
black kid, maybe sixteen)
stepped in the middle
and broke it up.

              He touched
my shoulder, then turned
back to where he'd been going,
resuming his distance, someone
I didn't know, who didn't know me.

"WHITE WOUND/BLACK SCAR"

SEEK Program, Queens College, 1969

for Arnold Kemp, wherever he is now

1

Despite being short I was "Lincoln Tall,"
the white liberal of your play
who confronts his bad dream (the unnamed
"Bum") on a bridge at night and talks himself
and his good intentions to death.
Bum clubs him down with a wine bottle,
condemning himself, by the act,
to be stuck there forever, since each
needs the other to get off the bridge.

But when we rehearsed it, Bum couldn't kill him
quickly enough for the brothers and sisters.
Each time Lincoln opened his mouth, even when
he struggled to fathom why
Bum was angry, they whistled him down.
Nothing I tried—a lowered voice, a tentative
awkwardness in his gestures—made any difference.
They jeered till the nightly breakaway bottle
bought on West Forty-seventh cracked on his head, and for them
the play ended there. Weeping and pacing the stage alone,
Bum delivered his epilogue. But his blow, struck
for all, wasn't his to take back.

The next day a student passed without speaking;
I asked her why. "It's that shit you say in the play."
"No, what *he* says in the play!
If I believed what he says, I wouldn't be in it."

On the train home, I tried to imagine
a black actor playing a serious role for an audience
that demanded a coon show.

2

Once, in a converted house on the edge of campus,
we rehearsed in the basement. Twilight massed
in the street-level window, making a one-way mirror.
Performance just two days away,
we got deep into the fight scene, cursing each other
with shouts of *honky* and *nigger*.
You head-butted me to the floor, pressed my shoulders
flat, while the right arm rained down punches.
A knock on the door stopped us. It was the cops.
"Someone saw you guys through the window
and called. What's going on?"
And at first they wouldn't believe us:
What better review could we want?

3

"Those images," you said, liking my new poem
better than I did. "Whenever I send something out
they take it, but I can't tell if it's good
or only the sort of thing they expect
a black writer to say." I thought of Bum's speech,
I was born black, I eat, drink, and sleep black,
I dream black and expect to die black
and go straight to black. Yes
that sort of thing. Was it also more?

4

Your South Bronx, the other pole
from my Hyde Park or its Lab School,
the U of Chicago's greenhouse, whose half-dozen blacks
spoke white English and scored 1500s

on the SAT. (In a story our lit mag printed,
a black child suffers his first
racist insult when he goes outside
still all aglow from his favorite record,
the Mozart horn concerti.)

After doing time for armed robbery,
you'd made your way here and made good.
The next stop, after a summer in Ghana
("You cannot believe the beauty here,"
your postcard said), was Harvard.
Then came a novel; its mixed notice
in the *New York Review;* then nothing.

5

Your play opened "SEEK Theatre Night,"
"The Last Poets" to follow. The audience now
was Poles and Italians who'd voted Nixon
for president, Proccacino for mayor—
the man who, speaking in Harlem, said,
"Believe me, my heart is as black as yours."

No catcalls now, just nervous silence.
Before, too much was funny, now nothing was.
It wasn't polite not to like it,
and they didn't like it. So they sat still.

For "The Last Poets," bristling with ritualized
rage and sexual boasting, they couldn't sit still.
With the chant of *A cunt is a cunt is a cunt,*
delivered with fist-pumping gestures,
a fight broke out in the audience.
What better review could they want?

6

Caught up in surviving the first semester
of graduate school, I didn't answer
your postcard from Ghana. I was relieved
to find a new miniature world like my high school,
where nothing would whack you
upside the head when your back was turned.
But my back *was* turned, and what it was turned on
happened whether I looked or not.
It was Lincoln's turn to be stuck on the bridge,
though I would have denied being stuck,
or being him, even. I still have your script.
Half a lifetime's under that bridge
since we parted ways. But if we met
on a street somewhere in New York,
I'd like to think we could play it again,
drawing bystanders and cops
into your bitter words that unsaid themselves
because we agreed to say them, and closed,
with its visible scar, an open wound.

OLD GRAVES IN BARBADOS

They thought they had
what they wanted, although
the stones of this Anglican churchyard,
flat to the ground where the trades
and the feet of the living erode
their names that we kneel to read,
say otherwise: the women
buried at thirty, joining the children
buried before them; the men
taken off by fever at forty
or killed in their twenties at sea.

Yet these were the masters,
not those who survived
a scant five years
from the hold
to an unmarked grave,

leaving behind
these faces, alive in the street,
whose gaze meets mine
not (as at home)
with offense taken
like poison, at last
spat back, but something
harder to translate,
like: *Please don't*
embarrass us with your shame,
which is after all useless.

DARK MATTER

Corot-green: already the green of earth. The mulch browns sober the brilliance of leaves still overhanging the soil below in their light-gapped canopy. They recognize kinship with what is below them; even in June, the dryness begins that will snap them free in October, driven earthward in rain. It is not the Monet-leaf, lit from within like cathedral glass, a thing of sky and air, as if the intelligence that made the lens of the eye were in what the eye sees, washing all in a common sea of scintilla. No, this is a nature that sleeps with its back to the light. It is not ourselves or what we would like to own of ourselves. Nothing mindlike rolls through its slates and browns.

Something to struggle with, as in the little-known oil in the Barnes Collection, where a fishing boat lies overturned on blocks on the beach, under stormlight, as we look toward a louring sea. It is either early morning or late afternoon, depending on where north is. Two men look intently at yellow-orange sparks from a welding torch as they seal the hull. That is the only brightness, the light of the mind amending dark matter. The boat will return to the sea, which will find a cracked seam in the weld, or a flaw in the caulker's pitch, or, finding none, make one of its own soon enough. We bail, weld, trust the hand's imperfect execution of the imperfect will.

THREE POEMS OF ELIJAH

1. His Calling

I lived as others do, avoiding death,
deploring evils I dared not oppose,
and making what I could of the distractions,
until I woke one morning with the words:
"There shall be neither rain nor dew these years
except according to my word; thus saith
the Lord"—and I, as one still sleeping, went
into the city, past the palace guard,
and into Ahab's presence, where I spoke
accordingly. The king was not more startled
than I was, coming to myself again
in the rasped hiss of suddenly drawn swords.
I fled, driven by voices, thought their thought,
not mine. But when I saw the widow chosen
to shelter me, I sighed with a young man's
disappointment, though I heard myself
declare that I could save her starving child.
She laughed uneasily, as if I'd said
the moon had fallen down the village well,
but beckoned me inside and, in the morning,
seeing her store of meal had been increased,
said I might stay. For days, no voices, save
these human ones, so full of gratitude.
Perhaps the Lord had used me only once;
might I not marry? True, the widow wasn't
beautiful—but young and, what's more, willing.
Her boy I liked at once, and told him stories,
embellishing my prophecy to Ahab
with hints of the king's death, and civil wars.
I dreamed of ordinary happiness,
and then one day I heard the widow call

the boy and get no answer. Silence; footsteps;
then her rising cry that filled the house.
I ran to see, and there the child lay,
fists clenched, eyes wide, as if to watch his soul
taking its last flight. I picked him up,
laid him on the bed in my own room,
and begged, in my own voice, this miracle.
The corpse's mouth fell open, and the breath
reentered it; but when I prayed, I chose
to serve the strangeness that had chosen me.

2. His Obedience

The fifty of them marching down the hill,
coming to summon me before the king—
all certitude and sunlight on their helmets,
with blank, symmetrical faces, as if formed
out of a single intention, not their own—
approached until their captain called a halt.
And while he droned his message, I began
to study them, until each face took on
a possible history. One I was sure
I knew, from neighborhoods that sheltered me,
and seeing the recognition in my eyes
was ill at ease. I'd passed him coming home
at evening, still in his uniform—
strikingly handsome, and he knew it too.
Women stole glances at him from the windows,
the children followed him and asked to hold
his shield, or touch the handle of his sword.

Once, a group of boys from pious households
threw stones at him, until I made them stop.
He thanked me, though reluctantly, the way
you'd thank an enemy for fighting fair.
I warned against false gods, but he replied,
"Whenever I meet a pretty girl, her god

is my god, for however long it takes."
He didn't fear his Maker's punishment
any more than a cat does, basking in sunlight.

Now the captain finished. I must answer.
As dice leap free of the closed hand came words:
If I be a man of God, let fire come down
from heaven and consume you and your fifty.
I had to speak this, knowing they'd be ash
as soon as it was out. And speak so no one
guessed I felt even a trace of pity.
I waited, staring at those unsuspecting
faces. Each stood out in its uniqueness,
irreplaceable. Then it was said.
They blazed, turned black, and dropped as bones—which ones
were whose? That night, I neither ate nor slept.
Even the thought of eating seemed obscene.
At daybreak, in the slant red of the sun,
came fifty soldiers, marching down the hill. . . .

3. His Unease in Heaven

This was three thousand years ago. At first
I could rejoice, sheltered beneath His arms.
But lately, as the dead arrived, I saw
how many were too young, how many led
small children by the hand, and could not comfort
either themselves or those who died with them.
They stared, uncomprehending, at His throne
as one might stare at sunlight in a drought.
And when I looked beyond the gate, I saw
a line of souls ascending, veiled in smoke,
through chimneys of the buildings far below.
Finally, one of the new arrivals spoke:
"O Lord, that made all things—the torturer,
the tortured, and the means of torturing—
often, in the garden by the house

they took me from, I thought, The flowers bloom
not knowing who I was that planted them;
but we, whom You made capable of knowledge,
why did You leave us in such ignorance?"
Turning his back once more on all the light,
he led the others to the crowded gate,
where they still keep their vigil, and their question.
Each spring at Passover, I walk the earth
until I find a likely looking house,
and watch the family seder through the window.
They pour the wine, though casually, as if
I'll never come for it. Only the children
quicken with the old anticipation,
hearing their father sing, *Elijah, come.* . . .
He rises, and he sets the door ajar.
O when will He Who Is That Which He Is
unlock the storehouse of the folded rainbow,
and bid me come to sit with them this night
that will not be like any other night,
drinking the heavy wine the living drink?

TO A FRIEND WHO CONCEDES NOTHING

You arrive, yes, but you bring your distance.
Even at parties—those tributes to the surface
(still intact, with its houses,
through aeons of rain and lightning)—your smile
looks hammered from something intractable,
long withheld from the sun. None of us
but descends in his time to the heart's forge
and bears some scar from its boiling metals.
But to *live* there, regarding the world
through cracks in its heavy door:
blinding sword blades of light, cleaned
of the transient objects they once carved.
For us, this comfort: that the place
must be bearable a moment longer,
since you are bearing it, indifferent
whether the work of your anvil rust in darkness
or shine at a stranger's hearth.

THE SPEED OF LIGHT

We were taught infinite patience
would see us through.
The woodcarver, hanging
first one thief, then the other,
at last the god in the middle—
each face, each minuscule
outstretched body
shaped to express
penitence, impenitence,
the cry of the ninth hour—
within the rosary bead, on crosses
measured and set to receive them.

But ask the painters
who made light live how long
the shadow will fill that hollow
under the model's cheekbone
before spilling formlessly out, as the sun
slides down and away. More volatile
than clouds twisting in flight,
this tryst of daylight and flesh.

While the raised hand considers,
it vanishes. Dip now
in the swift current circling
from things to the eye:
save what you can.

LATE ARRIVAL

If, steadily, this ray of light
that left its star before the eye
that sees it was conceived,

and might have ended
in any of the windows,
too numerous to count,
in any of the houses
whose lights stretch farther
than the eye can follow,

or missed all houses altogether,
dropping into a tree
outside, the empty street,
unpopulated woods or desert,
drowned between two islands
in the mid-Pacific,
lost with Scott on the polar icecap—

swallowed down a crater of the moon,
shining into a grain of sand
on Mars, or ended
nowhere at all, unreeling
into unsounded space—

and having found, by a chance
too slim to calculate, my window,
must find my eye
as I turn my head a moment
to see if the sky is clear,

and not choose the white,
the iris, but
the sentient lens—

If this has reached me,
who is to say my thoughts
are unknown to You?

YOU ARE HERE

There is no name for the *dread* in my *heart*—which both
sound hopelessly wrong, like a valveless
horn no one plays anymore, except
to make composers like Bach sound strange.
Too strange already, I'd have thought, outdoing
the best of us, helped by something broken
past repair, if not dissolved entirely away:
cruder instruments then, but finer music.
For us, no mighty fortress, its walls a limit
we could live in, not yet paralyzed with yearning.

Only the sun, that leaves us alone at nightfall,
the sky above us filling up with stars.

        ✳

On one of my T-shirts, a spiral galaxy with an arrow
pointing to one of its outermost arms, and the words:
YOU ARE HERE. And you are if you think so.

I wear it to the gym, where four times a week
I run in circles and strain against machines
to strengthen this heart, where the dread is,
and postpone its end. On my other shirts,
defiant boasts (AS I GOT OLDER, I GOT BETTER),
jock celebrations (CHICAGO BULLS: WORLD CHAMPIONS)
that don't console. They scarcely address

what I see when, unable to sleep,
I get up and walk about in my house:

the light from streetlamps
working unwearied through the blinds,
my wife's face, known at a glance from all others,
profiled on the pillow.

To the cat, wound in a ball,
nothing matters beyond that sphere.

✳

On my T-shirt, it scarcely matters: house, city, nation,
planet, solar system, Proxima Centauri,
honed to an arrow's point, all "here." What, scaled so large,
is absence? My father, dead these thirty years,
has just stopped speaking, his voice hangs in the air.
My daughter, nine hundred miles away at college,
is down the hall, no farther than her room.
No need of this picture, where she looks pensively
into the camera that stands in for me and her mother
who look with it into her eyes and wish her home.

To see on that scale is possible
a moment, but we're too small to sustain it.

✳

Still at a loss to improve on *dread,*
I know it's not in the *heart* (having stood exhausted
and sleepless in this diffused light). It's in the nerves,
a namelessness that can't be worn
on any shirt. It circulates,
as blood does, through the smallest capillary.
I feel it as itching on my eyelids when they close,
as noise from the apartment opposite

that startles me bolt upright. As runaway thought-trains
gathering speed all night, derailed toward morning.

*

Having trained for a duel
with some presence fit to kill or be killed by,
I'm helpless against this absence—
or, worse, this night filled with passing voices
from all directions at once.

Had neither succeeded in killing the other,
we might still have agreed to circle
around each other, defining a single axis.

Too late for that gyroscope now, when I'm shaken by everything,
sure that each voice, while I hear it, ought to be followed,
backed with violence against all enemies.

Even a ghost needs blood to finish its job:
unquiet spirit, it seems we both want to kill.

Shall I offer the use of my hands?

*

Well, Dad: smoking two packs a day didn't do it.
The bourbon poured on the ulcer didn't,
or going stark mad and turning your hair, what was left of it,
white in a year; not the strange foods—
the potted iguana, fried grasshoppers, anything *tref* on offer—
not two wrenching divorces, or months of lassitude
punctured by fitful tennis. Not the demands of your patients,
spilling their guts till you didn't know theirs from your own,

letting them call at all hours; not even the furious
whipsaw of downers and uppers, hauling you in and out of sleep.
Accidentally-on-purpose waits on accident; impatient,
you took an enormous dose of the nearest way.

✷

In the lit windows across the street live others
sneaking a look at lit windows and singing,
with Schubert's jilted wanderer,
Du fändest Ruhe dort—

✷

As I start for home with my nose in the paper,
one of the beggars who loiters beside the newsstand
on Sunday mornings asks, in her monotone, for change.
Last week I gave it, this week I withhold.

The light pours like a flash flood, filling Main Street,
where inmates of the old hotel turned stopping place
for the cracked past mending or congenitally miswired
stroll in bleached-out primary colors; pointing or muttering
to no one visible, they take the air.

✷

With breakfast cleared, the faces of interned Haitians,
buildings on fire in Los Angeles, shelled flat in Sarajevo,
go on the pile for recycling. Like the coffee
we sipped while taking them into awareness,
they begin to wear off, till nothing is left
but a thin haze of unease one feels almost at home in.

I escape to the comics, the number-heaven
of sports . . . the light, now perceptibly slanted,
at rest in the garden.

✴

Two among many dangers set for the devious survivor
of seafaring and war:
                    rocks that converge and smite
the enemy's otherness flat;

                        also the whirlpool
that pulls you toward the rocking sleep of ocean,
until the two-note ground bass,
wave/trough, wave/trough,
accompanies only itself, having swallowed
all sentient voices, and you and the sea are one.

But rocklike vigilance
is a form of sleep,
unconscious of what shatters on its wall;
the sleep at the end of the whirlpool
a form of vigilance, the unstillable
swing of the sea's hammer, rising and falling.

✴

I pull from my shelf Cantata 80, *Ein' Feste Burg,*
and play it, front door open, into the street:

the singers belt it like Verdi,
the trumpets and drums dubbed in by Wilhelm Friedemann
ring out their purely inauthentic joy.

But the street keeps answering: cars like pulsars
drifting in from deep space (back wheels
jacked up, bazooka speakers,
amplifiers that would fill a stadium)
shiver the joists of the house.

REFRACTION OF WORDS
OVERHEARD IN THE STREET

*"I wonder if people who matter ever think
that people who don't matter . . ."*

No one is still alive
who planted the trees above us,
about to come into leaf.

He and the man he talks with
are in their forties, bearded,
and still have most of their hair.

Under his feet, the ants
cut winding tunnels. Beetles
stir in their nest of roots.

Shadows of branches quiver
in wind. You can discern
each brick in the garden wall,

etched by the sharp March sunlight.
It looks as if each one matters,
unless none of them does.

VIRGO

Under her gaze, the summer opens, closes.
She holds a rod of germinated grain
When there is no grain yet in nature, only
Patches of melting snow broken with stubble.
Low in the east, toward morning, she will watch
What lovers do on blankets stretched across
The summer grass, and be no warmer for it.
She knows where summer is going, as she drifts
West, against her reckoning with the sun.
She meets him when the thunderheads begin
To rise in the afternoons, like continents
Climbing free of the sea. Beneath the rifts,
The sunlit air ranges itself in towers.
Nothing looks more certain to dissolve;
Nothing looks more solid. We wait, our houses
Shrouded in rain, and when the rain is gone,
She goes, folds up the summer like a fan.

HOMAGE TO WEBERN

Your music lasts three hours—a lifework pent
inside one Mozart opera. Each note leans
into the next with a panicked urgency
that would have seemed, to Mozart's audience,
surrender to the unredeemed condition
music heals by giving every moment,
through relation to the rest, a sweetness
it had lacked alone. But here, relation
means anticipating when the brutal
interval, the interrupting silence
comes, as someone in the woods at night
might trip and, knowing he had lost the path,
guess from his accident where it must be.
Born since your death, we learn to hear the heart
not as a rhythm deep inside the body
urging us outward to our loves and wars,
but as mind's object, HERE BE MONSTERS scrawled
across the very center of the map.
Your music ends as we're afraid we'll end:
the pattern secretly completes itself
before we understand it, leaving us
to ask whose will we did, if not our own.

VICISSITUDES OF ORPHEUS

The legend of Orpheus as peerless musician concerns the early part of the tale, when the trees follow him and the beasts drop the torn prey from their jaws to listen. Not yet paired with Eurydice, he is immersed in his own being, toward which all else can't help but turn. To us who listen, the tale depicts his music as an art of power: it will make him loved—by men and women, by animals, by sentient but unconscious foliage, by the insensate stones themselves. With the coming of Eurydice, he is no longer a presence open to all, within whose music all may come and go as casually as strollers in a park, without violating the utter self-enclosure which is the source of its delight. There, the stones could hang weightless, the trees drift free of their roots. Now, his singing is given to someone. It emanates from him like a beam of light directed toward her.

Eurydice cannot refuse him. He will not be required to step out of his music and seek her; he sings and she comes unbidden to his side. And might remain there, into deep uneventful old age, except that the snake, responding snake fashion to warm-blooded flesh crossing its field, strikes her and kills. Within the zone of his music, this could not have happened. But he is away with the young men as she prepares for the wedding among the young women. The field has been silent for hours.

He has lived long enough to see that the dead stay dead, no matter how deeply we love them. But if nature itself has left its nature under the spell of his song, who is to say that he cannot sing back the dead?

If Eurydice had not already begun to change him, he would have sat, indifferent, beside the door to the underworld, letting his song drift down to Persephone and Hades, throned under the strata, locked in the self-consoling music of his grief. But in the painful lack of her presence, he begins to understand the idea of limit, of walls between lover and beloved. She is elsewhere, veiled by the darkness stretching unsounded beneath him. When he descends, he is frightened, and fear will change the timbre of what he sings. He aims his song at Hades and Persephone, in whose power it lies to open a door in the limit. That is why Monteverdi makes his aria, *possente spirto,* a virtuoso showpiece, more impressive but less moving than the farewell to the earth that begins his descent. (And lets him waste it, too, on stone-eared Charon, in whom the song induces not preternatural wakefulness but sleep.) Orpheus steals unhindered over the Styx. All light fails in crossing that river; the death realm, remorseless as a hyperdense star, pulls it back. Beyond, on the unseen shore, the all-gathering ear of Hades attends to the song, and the glacially slow sliding of flesh toward his realm. A germination stirs in the husk-heart of Persephone, since overhearing is more poignant than direct address.

It is a half success. The god is not so moved as to melt his sovereignty altogether into the music. He is still in office, making conditions, contracts, which are a limit of sorts. For him, too, it is a question of power. Death is the law on which his domain is founded, and he means to enforce it strictly. What Orpheus, blinded by hope and fear, cannot see is the motive, why the god offers, along with the gift, its means of undoing.

Here the scholars diverge. Some hold that the god is playing a game. It is dull in the underworld; no result is uncertain with dead people, whose possibilities were exhausted during their lives. To bet on a living man's resolve, unsure of the outcome, may be the only unforeclosed act open to him through all eternity.

Others are sure the god knows, when he makes the condition, that Orpheus cannot comply. He will obey his nature and turn around.

No one loves a death god, but try doing without one. He has the hard task of arming desire to bear itself within necessity, to learn that one day what it loves will not come back. But he does more: he teaches Orpheus a truth of his art. For the zone of power where his music binds the listener is a liminal place, like the dark margin between the god's kingdom of stasis and the threshold of the earth turning in its seasons; like the blue line of the horizon, retreating before the sail; like the round theater of dreams where the dead return. In his singing, she returns but cannot step over the threshold into his arms. It is not enough, but it is what he may have.

To the living he seems as he was before her coming, entirely withdrawn in himself, secreting a zone of impersonal music. They are slow to perceive that it is a sealed space now, which none but Eurydice is invited to enter. Her death has sprouted new intervals, bitter as nettles, in the path of his voice. Notes that had never been struck at once cluster under his fingers, their overtones biting the air like the teeth of a saw. The Bacchae, listening, sense the privacy of the music, which in their principled hatred of boundaries they are obliged to violate. They drown him out with a battery of percussion, hammering crude symmetrical time on the stretched hides of beasts, hollowed blocks of cypress and oak. They pull his music into the general dance of flesh, so that it cannot strike out alone into the darkness between the two worlds, where Eurydice may or may not be listening, if she has not left her hearing behind with her body.

But they will do more: they will pull apart the boundary that separates him from what is not himself, the contours of his face, the vein-map in his forearms, the living waters of his eyes, and the inward spaces behind them, the finely tuned chambers in which the head-tones are formed before he releases them into the air. Everything secret they will have out, and everything uniquely named by his name, such that seeing him or hearing him from however great a distance we know him as Orpheus, they will merge into the All. Their nails delve in his flesh; they rock his head this way and that until, like a boulder dislodged from its nest in the earth, it rolls free of his body. The column of air from diaphragm to larynx, which is the shape his music takes before it departs its formative silence, is severed, never to be made whole. His blood leaps free on the wind at last, while the head falls into the river, sliding since its inception toward the sea. The head, its throat precariously intact, obeys its deep imperative to sing, the waves of sound formed half from the rippling water, half from the eddying air. Once all nature followed him, but now only jackdaws and corbies, forming a black river in space that doubles the serpent's course of the waters below.

There is nothing left for him to want, and only the minimal fragment of the "I" that wanted it; were any less of him left, the song would lack the means to go on, and even now the river is rushing toward the sea, where the sharks will silence him, stripping his skull to the same shade of white as those of the countless mariners drowned before him. Among the crania of illiterate seamen and their tone-deaf officers, his own will make one, picked clean as theirs, impossible to distinguish even were someone to dive in the hope of retrieving some reliquary shard.

Along the banks of the river, the trees shrink back toward the forest behind them; the animals burrow into their dens and stop their ears. What they hear is intolerable; those unable to flee will be stone-deaf for the rest of their lives. Only the men and women who dwell in the isolated villages downstream are able to bear it. Though most have been stolid peasants, eking subsistence out of an alkaline soil after the way of their forebears, their lives are broken in half from this day. They become makers of ballads, wandering from town to town, their sparse possessions slung on their backs; they ship for voyages of exploration and settle in uncharted lands where their journals dissolve in tropical rains; they interpret the dreams of kings who break them on the rack for prophesying famine, pestilence, humiliation under the boots of conquerors.

II

MEDITATIONS ON THE FIELD MUSEUM

1

The fountain
is the only thing that moves.
Is flowing unbroken since my childhood
when I came here with my father who is dead
and moves in my mind only.

2

"How high is the ceiling?"
I asked my father, looking
past his face
and through the skeleton of Gorgosaurus
to the distant skylights.
A hundred feet?
He said it was more like fifty.
As we walked into the steady rain
that had been falling since breakfast,
I thought the afternoon would last forever;
the marble steps glistened, the lake
was sleeping under the fog.
I was eight, and he was forty
with seven years to go.

3

The height of the ceiling in the Field Museum
is eighty-five feet.

4

I felt lost in the basement
but found my way by color
to the mummy room:
dim-lit green corridors
with models of Paleolithic caves;
the bright red Coke machine,
my father's height,
meant it was near—
then through the door to the chamber

of dead kings, lit and clothed in gold.
Some of the little coffins
not my size, eyebrows
raised in permanent astonishment.
On one of the faces, the gold
was chipped away.
I looked at my father,
who put his hands in his pockets,
sternly unmoved.
He didn't like it either, I could tell.

5

I watch my daughter's face
on her first visit
for signs of the old fear,
but she is all dry-eyed wonder,
asking, matter-of-fact,
"Are all the animals dead in here?"
Her favorites are the artists' reconstructions:
the panorama of a Permian swamp,
the plaster trilobites and life-sized cavemen—
not the bones and restitched animals.

6

So I went down alone, with a notebook,
to see what it was that had got to me.
The basement had been redone,
all glass and off-white paint
like the lobby of a Mies apartment complex.
The mummies lay in a long line,
propped up slightly, as if recuperating.
I wrote their names and dynasties.

A field trip, tended by two
blond and intensely suburban teachers,
arrived, and I hung back to listen.
Two children, eight or nine years old,
stopped suddenly at a plain wood coffin
housing the bodies of twins.
"Ooh," said one, "that's real."
"Look," said one of the teachers
in that perky chirp that washes off unpleasantness,
"there's a mommy,
and this one's a child."

I leaned my notebook on a stone sarcophagus,
1300 B.C. and cold
to the heel of my hand.

7

It's no good, Mr. Field.
Not that it isn't impressive:
the Greek proportions, the marble
looming up white from the lake
which might pass, on a clear day,
for the Mediterranean.

The pharaohs glitter;
the animals stand in midstride
and turn to the visitor
preternaturally wakeful eyes;
the elephant drives his tusk
in his rival's hide
for wondering children.
And the bust of you on the stairway stares
at the Absolute, with a grim faith
impervious to irony.

8

The illusion holds this afternoon
as I walk through the north doors
with my wife and daughter.
Rain has dimmed the skylights.
This is the timelessness of the other world,
its diffuse glow of spirit
that neither begins nor ends;
the low hiss of the fountain, susurrus,
indwelling voice.
The shells and bones
of animals no man has seen alive
are gathered here, where nothing
that once had life dies utterly.
I think of my own death:
my soul in a glass case somewhere,
aboveground, seeing and seen.
I think of my father and he emerges
from the adjoining hall, and glides near.
He looks a long time at the two faces
he didn't live to see.
If I spoke their names he could not hear me.
But he looks less troubled and retires
around the corner, into the shadows.
I could believe it this afternoon.

9

Though all its architecture strains
toward permanence,
it warns us everywhere:
Here where you stand was water once,
as these bones witness.
And the wall of ice that gouged the lakes
will walk again,
the sun and north wind
set up a nervous give-and-take in these walls;
and beneath the marble floor
waits the black earth,
devourer of forms.

10

Oh who will remember the banded peccary,
the keel-backed turtle, the blue-tongued skink,
the racket-tailed drongo,
the leaf-nosed bat?
When the earth breaks on its axis,
who shall plead for the whale-headed stork,
the disk-fingered gecko, the short-eared phalanger,
the "sluggish, arboreal" spotted cuscus?
Who will call you, Hormahes and Peptah,
Harwah, Menhotep, and Itefib, oldest
of these human dead?
They wait, toughing it out upright,
names safe at their feet,
until the angel with the face of a fox
and the hands of a man unlock them,
and they scatter in the jungle which is God.

MY FATHER'S FATHER
BEFORE HIM

1951

Had he snapped like a dried moth
when I hugged him, I'd have said,
"Of course."
His three-piece suits had pinstripes
so fine they disappeared in the black cloth.
Only the gold chain of his pocketwatch
had light or color, the face
too pale to have blood in it.
Something had gone out
in the eyes. They were done
with looking.
          Absently
he gave out presents,
denying us
nothing. It was Mother
who told him to stop
while you said nothing.

He came from Toronto. How polar,
how sunless, must that city be
to make such skin and such eyes!
I still mistype it
"Toronot"—abode of nonbeing,
your birthplace and secret home.

Those hot summer evenings, the grill
smoking with meat, your friends
stood around in shorts and short sleeves.
You laughed too much and too loudly,
sprung from Toronot till they went home.

OPENING SPACES

1. The Window

Sun striking the building tops at eye level;
below, as at a mountain's foot, the lake
gathered offshore in swells, then suddenly reared
to strike the breakwaters. In our binoculars
appeared the latticed catwalks of freighters
and metal ladders climbing the concrete walls
of islandlike water purification plants.

2. The Locks

Hot summer days, our boat rides on the river
gave us the city as the river sees it,
threaded through openwork bridges, flung vertical
into the sun. Then we paused in the locks:
the walls kept growing higher, as in a dream,
till only the iron ladders by the sluice gate
and the faint discolored line, far overhead,
drawn by decades of water lapping on concrete,
gave reassurance we'd climb out again.

3. The Freightyard

You used to hold me over the concrete wall
that overlooked the tracks so I could watch
the freight trains heading for the open plains.
One time, a policeman made you put me down:
Too dangerous, he said. Though nothing but
your arms around my waist stopped me from falling,
I well remember: I was not afraid.

SCENES FROM CHILDHOOD

1. Their Quarrel

Her anger pierced
their bedroom door.
I heard all her words.

His reply seeped under,
a silted river,
burdened, opaque.

Her forgiveness, a bell
sure that it rings
pure law, pure justice.

2. Their House

Don't they know
the house is alive?

How can they call me
out of the sunlight

into its mouth?
At night it threatens

to grind me apart—
I will live on as pieces.

What use to stroke
my hair and say,

You can become
whatever you want?

ESTES PARK

1956

1

On the high plateau, sagebrush
hid the ground, pocked with prairie-dog holes,
that stretched to the feet of the nearest mountains
twenty miles off, though they looked close.

The scale outleapt imagination:
Pikes Peak and Longs Peak,
treeless stone, snowcaps, and scarves of cloud
etched against purest blue. At night
stars limned the mountains' teeth in sparks.
Dim ones I knew, third or fourth magnitude,
outshone the swarm around them,
while Deneb, Altair, and Vega
blazed like Jupiter. The Milky Way, invisible
from our city, stretched like a bridge of phosphorus
arching from south to north
where the jaws of the mountains swallowed it
in absolute blackness . . . frame of the teeming sky.

2

Days, we climbed the more modest ones
whose names did not end in "peak," Twin Sisters
the only one that took us above the timberline.
The air was fragrant with pines,
suddenly cut with horsedung.
You showed me how to find north by the moss
on the shadowed side of trees. We rested by lakes,

deep as Superior in the narrow
hollows glaciers had gouged there,
the melted waters potable and clear.
They looked like their names:
Emerald, Crystal, Silver.

3

The archery targets leaned
against massive bales of hay, to catch
stray arrows of children and rank beginners.
I wanted the most resistant bow I could bend.

(Playing catch with you, I had noticed how far
the ball sailed in the mountain air, and how the curve
that had just begun to break that spring was not breaking here.)

My arrows flew far and wild.

HOME

It will take time, your postcard says, but you will get better.
You miss us; moreover the food where you are is terrible.
It is boring there, with nothing to do but read and wait.
For me and my sister, postcards, but sealed letters to Mother—
one of which, unsealed to me thirty years later, said:
The harm done me, and done by me, has gone too far.
We should kill the kids in their sleep to spare them suffering,
then kill ourselves and be done.

Once, during your stay in the hospital, I sat in the sunroom,
until my attention wandered from the backyard's
red fence, single flourishing maple, garage, and swings
to the curtain. The sun shone through the weave of bright orange,
yellow, and apple green, making each thread transparent.
I saw how the colors crossed and meandered
jaggedly sideways, then returned to their course.
I stared, it must have been several minutes, at where
one green and one orange thread met, twined, and parted.
I memorized the shape of that crossing, then tried
to take in a larger pattern, a whole square inch at once—
as if pulling this small domain into my consciousness
would save my life. When I closed my eyes,
I could not recall it. The sun was falling behind
the house across the alley, and soon the curtain would be in shadow.
I pulled back my gaze to the scale of the room,
and saw how tiny the realm that defeated me was.

3

We left on a sudden "vacation," and you came home to an empty house.
To my sister and me, it seemed unnaturally cruel.
We returned to find you waiting for us, alone.
It was overcast, late afternoon, but no lights were on.
When you raised your face from your hands I was frightened:

your hair was almost gone, and what remained
was the white of extreme old age. Your skin (pale,
smooth) looked friable, like your father's.
Your eyes moved no more than a blind man's—
they took nothing in and gave nothing back.
Your shoulders pulled forward and in, so the body
I used to be proud to inherit, compact and powerful,
looked too compact, too dense, as if some enormous weight
had been pulled inside
and would never get out.

I had read about stars, how the sun would shine steadily
for millions of years and then swell to the size of Antares,
swallowing all of its planets closer than Jupiter,
and then collapse to a pale dwarf of itself,
pulling the matter around it down and in. Later,
they would discover black holes that could bend light
from its path and never release it.

                    When you finally spoke
I could scarcely hear you, the voice was so listless
and indistinct, as if the words formed
in the back of your throat never touched tongue or lips.

A VISIT

1959

On that half-lit
sunken floor,
the whiskey glowed,
like a banked ember
in faceted glass.
You poured one drink,
then another
till your face smoldered,
darkened to ash;

you rehearsed the woes
of your second divorce.
Our hostess, your patient
once, did all
the listening now,
judgment suspended
an expanded hour.

Were they close friends,
these people I met
that night, just once?
And why was I there?

Her multiple sclerosis
had begun to show,
you said, though
she looked normal.

Her heavyset husband
said almost nothing,
rising to pour
another whiskey
and drop back into
his chair's deep leather—
a year later,
I read in the paper
that he'd been indicted
for some sort of fraud.

But all the cops
must have been asleep
when you drove home:
red light after red
light ignored,
as other lights
shot past like meteors.
You drove at anger's
light-quick speed:

What did a woman
want from a man,
and how many times
did she want it, and why
did she want so much of it
so many times
each night, each week?

You dropped me home;
unhurt, I stared
at myself in the mirror,
thinking I must be
injured somewhere.
Yes, but where?
I went to bed.

From that night on,
I would dream you
arcing through space,
tranced on the glowing
instrument dials,
embarked past no
return, on no road,
into the frigid
void between stars.

FIRST KISS

Indian Hill, 1960

Her name was Phyllis, like the shepherdesses
in the madrigals. She had a throaty voice
and sang the alto solos in chorus. She taught me
bawdy catches. We were kids
but the songs knew everything.

In the free hour of darkness before the counselors
counted boys and girls in separate beds,
we slipped into the gazebo by the floodlit pool
for our first kiss. That hour has become
a place, holding its shape against time,

except that her quickened breathing
under my hands clasped on her back,
the quiver that passed from her voice
through my palms when she said,
"I love you too,"

have gone and cannot return.
Gone too the orange and red glow
of the Japanese lanterns, broken in liquid arcs
on the nightlit pool, the ripples shifting,
never to find the same pattern again.

KEEPSAKE

1962

It seemed impossible to move my face,
which hung there numb. And those who knew my father
before I had my chance to know him said,
"You won't remember how he had us roaring;
everyone says he should have been an actor."

I tried to think of my father having them roaring.
A picture of him, young, in a straw hat,
shows him leaning proudly on his car
giving his profile to the camera
as people do who think themselves attractive.
He's handsomer than his three friends; the sun
catches the wavy blond hair on his temples.
He might have had them roaring, I don't know.

There is no picture of my father leaving
our house on Crandon. Scarcely on his feet,
each arm draped on the shoulders of a friend,
he mumbled an inaudible good-bye
and nodded, meaning he was ready, as
their dark suits filled the doorway, then descended
into the bright spring day, and down the walk.
I must have watched him go: I have this picture.

RÉSUMÉ

Leaving behind such scattered facts as these:
Born 1914, of Jewish refugees

From some pogrom near Kiev. The name may be
Some Irish customs officer's legacy,

The nearest Old Sod, New World allophone
For the mumbled Russian. Yet, from that day on,

The Russian name became almost taboo,
Like mention of the past it pointed to.

The grandfather, a doctor, drove his son
To follow him and study medicine

(Although, as someone at the funeral said,
He should have taken acting up instead).

Discouraged with neurology, which was
"The study of incurable disease,"

He planned to be a psychoanalyst.
(One sees the balked artistic bent in this,

But if he hoped for cure, then his new plan
Exchanged the fire for the frying pan.)

He married, did his residency at Penn—
No hospital in Canada would hire Jews then—

Yet, came the war, when Canada declared,
He went back north at once and volunteered

For combat. But they wouldn't let him go
And kept him stationed in Ontario.

(His colonel, he learned later, shared the views
Of German colonels, when it came to Jews.)

His skills were in request behind the lines:
The army, to induce young men to join,

Had offered every volunteer a choice:
One might "go active," or serve otherwise.

And so, whole regiments were overrun
By men who never meant to fire a gun.

Having outfoxed itself, the military
Tried intimidation. "Coward! Fairy!"

—Thus shirkers were addressed, as if by name.
They slept in yellow tents. When morning came,

They crawled on gravel, on their hands and knees,
Fitted with yellow armbands, or were left to freeze

For hours, standing naked at attention.
But none chose combat to escape detention,

And he, who had not been allowed to go,
Was called upon to say why this was so.

After a week in which I interviewed
Nearly a thousand men, I must conclude

They never will go active. If you ask them why,
They'll tell you simply, "I don't want to die"—

A motive I find eminently sane.
(His expertise would not be sought again.)

✷

In two split seconds, two unthinkable bombs
Buckled Japan; the newsreel catacombs

Of Auschwitz, Belsen, Dachau, Buchenwald,
Gave up their dead, and living-dead. Appalled,

The nations shuddered briefly . . . then once more
Began sleepwalking down the path to war.

And yet for now, he thought, the world was safe.
Because he knew that any child's life

Would end in Hitler's ovens, if Hitler won,
He'd waited to have children. He was done

With waiting now, impatient to begin
Making a future. . . .
                              That's where I came in.

THE RETURN

Children never catch up: I will always move
in a world torn by your earlier passage.
You have gone deep into the mountains
to live as a recluse, until I am ready to join you.

But we were together there
in the timeless, spaceless point
that brought time and space out of itself
and made us, each in our time, after the time allotted
the trilobite, the dinosaur, the megatherium.

The fern leaf on the coal face, the dragonfly
soaring in its amber bead, the ammonite's stone coils
annealed in shards on the seafloor, all limbs
of one body—animal, vegetable, and mineral at once—
expanding its forms in space, which itself flies
forever outward, void supplanting profounder void.

Unless the outward rush
is a bungee jump, and the unseen cord
snaps suddenly taut: the galaxies
head home to the hole in space, in time,
that threw them forth. And what, by the merciful
separation of space, was private, and what,
by the merciful separation of time, was healed,

must lie together where there is no separation,
each being, each moment interpenetrating all others
more profoundly than the most impassioned lovers.
Even the medieval carvers who crowded
the Crucifixion and its turbulent onlookers
into a single rosary bead never imagined
this vanishing point, where mocker and crucified
become each other and nothing, end without world.

IN A ROWBOAT, ONCE, BY NIGHT

The water lapping below the gunwale scattered
moonlight in broken arcs, all the way to the pier
shadowed below the pines (you could smell the pines
out on the water). Even with the moon
near full, you could see the Milky Way's
hazed band descend to the black, massed trees.

I was twelve. Don, my favorite counselor,
sat in the bow—the one who taught me chess
so he'd have someone to beat. Who answered
my questions about girls, until he'd heard
enough: "Let's talk about *women*."
Who said he played jazz saxophone
(but not for us) and knew
where all the stars and constellations were.

The oars made such a liquid sound, folding the water.
Who would want to be anywhere else?
And then these voices, two men talking low
on the beach, somewhere off in the darkness,
floated across the water to where we glided,
a half mile out. It was as if there were bridges
stretching over the lake, connecting everyone,

and across years, so the sky
fills with stars again, ringed by the trees,
as the boat is sliding across that lake
whose name I have forgotten. I hear
the stroke of the oars, those calm, impersonal voices,
saying I have forgotten what,
folding me into their promise that the night is still,
the fathers awake, watching over their children,
that the night is still, and clear, and long.